BOOST YOURSELF

How you can create the very best version of yourself as a kid

NICK SHAHRYARI

ISBN: 978-1-09837-497-6

A message from the author:

This is a practical and straight-to-the-point book about how to boost your life. I made sure to keep this book super simple and to not bore you with unnecessary text. I know some books can be extremely boring to read, when writing this book I set out to make sure this is not one of them.

How to read this book:

Read this book with a pen or highlighter in hand so you can highlight, circle, or underline any part of the book you think is important! Come back to this book if you ever need to! And take notes on any part you feel is important!

Why I wrote this book:

Imagine if most kids were like this:

- Addicted to vaping or smoking weed
- Sleeping only a few hours every night

- Not able to focus and get work done
- Hanging around troublemaker kids who bring them further away from their goals

Now imagine if most kids were like this:

- Never doing any recreational drugs
- Getting the recommended amount of sleep
- Able to focus and get work done
- Hanging around good friends who are encouraging

Let me tell you the story of two friends (the names have been changed for this story). Bob and Bill were childhood friends since elementary school. Both of them have big dreams for their lives and are excited about their futures. One day they go to a party while they're in high school. At the party, they get offered drugs. Bob decides to try the drugs, and Bill decides not to try the drugs and leaves the party. Over the next few months, Bob continues to use drugs and try new ones while Bill spends his time avoiding drugs and working on making his dreams come true. Ten years later, Bob ends up homeless and addicted to drugs while Bill becomes super successful. What can we learn from this story? Bob never grew up wanting to become a drug addict. He grew up wanting to be successful, he had big dreams, but because he decided to try drugs once, he fell into a lifetime of addiction, never achieving his big goals.

I wrote this book to prevent as many people as possible from falling into the wrong path of using drugs, having bad habits, and hanging around the wrong people. In most cases, people don't fall into the wrong path on purpose. It happens by accident. When you're in school, it can be especially easy to fall into the wrong path with all the distractions out there. In this book, I talk about things you can do so that you don't accidentally fall into the wrong path.

.

Chapter 1:

My Story

My name is Nick Shahryari. My self-improvement journey started in the 8th grade after stumbling upon the book How to Win Friends and Influence People by Dale Carnegie. After reading the book, I was surprised about many things. I was surprised that I read the entire book. I had never read a chapter book from start to finish until then. I thought I was a really bad reader, so I used to avoid reading books. I realized the reason why I read the book cover to cover because I was so interested in the topic of the book, self-development. I learned that when you are interested in a certain book's topic, reading it becomes a lot easier. I used to think all chapter books were boring before reading this book. It was so interesting to me that you could make yourself a better person overall through self-development.

After finding self-help, I improved myself. I took what I learned from the book and became better at socializing with others, focusing, getting the right amount of sleep, and just had a whole lot of excitement that I could make myself an upgraded person overall. I feel like there's a lot of people that are not in the best situation right now but could improve it through self-help. Maybe, someone is feeling hopeless, having trouble focusing, and not hanging out with the best people. If that is you, I am glad you are reading this book. I think you will find this book very helpful.

In this book, I talk about:

- Focusing
- Learning
- Life
- Social media
- Sleep
- Friends
- Hope
- And drugs

Get ready. This is some really good stuff that can change your life.

Chapter 2

Focus, Learning, and Life

When you think about it, you realize that as a kid, all you really have is time. That's your main advantage. And if you don't use your time in the best way possible, that can lead to a wasted life and wasted potential. So you need to get serious about using your time in the best way possible. And when I'm saying you need to use your time in the best way possible, I'm saying that you have to make choices that will pay off in the long run. Sometimes, that choice could be to go to a concert with a group of friends because it'll make a great memory. Other times it can be to give your complete focus to studying for a big test. It can also be to delete all your social media to free up time to work on a business idea. Wasting time is what ruins many people's lives. And in today's world, we have a lot of distractions, so it can be hard to focus. Use the strategies below to give yourself a time advantage. Think of using what I'm talking about below as a cheat code to life.

Being able to focus is an essential skill that can help you use your time in the very best way possible. What would I recommend you do the next time you need to focus? The Pomodoro Technique is my favorite. Here's how it works:

First, put your distractions somewhere you can't see. The further away, the better. Usually, these distractions are electronic devices like phones. Or give your distractions to a family member instead of you putting it somewhere. If you choose to do this way, tell the family member not to give the device back until you're done with whatever you are doing. It's important that there are no distractions nearby.

Set a timer for 25 minutes. It's always better to use a classic timer instead of an internet one. If you use an internet timer, you could get distracted by your phone, tablet, computer, etc.

When the timer goes off, take a 5-minute break.

Repeat if needed.

If you're still not done with whatever you're doing after four cycles of this, take a longer 15-30 minute break, then restart the process.

Extra tip: If you feel like the focusing is going well after the timer rings, you don't have to take a break. You can continue until you're completely done with whatever you're doing.

Sometimes it can be hard to actually sit down and start the Pomodoro Technique. When thinking about doing something like homework, one of the most common things people say to themselves is, "I'll do that homework later." A simple mind trick that works for me is to tell myself that "I will procrastinate later." For example, "I'll watch YouTube videos later after I finish this homework." Before I start the Pomodoro Technique, I like to go on YouTube and find a few videos I want to watch. I save those videos to my "watch later" playlist then I get to work. This really motivates me to finish whatever I am doing since I know there is a reward ready when I am finished.

Adding to the Pomodoro Technique, get some exercise/physical activity too. Even a 10-minute jog could help your brain to focus better and work harder. Exercise can be amazing for the brain and body. Try to add exercise into your life if it's not already. The possibilities for different kinds of exercise are endless by searching up different workouts on the internet!

Some benefits of exercise:

- Improved mood
- A boost in energy
- Better overall sleep

The social media problem:

Almost all of us have been there, scrolling through social media platforms for hours upon hours just to realize there's a ton of homework due the next day, and you still haven't started. This is called procrastination, and it can definitely be one of the worst things you could do for yourself. Procrastinating can leave you with a ton of stress and anxiety. Avoid procrastination since it's better to finish whatever you have to do and then relax. This way, you can feel more relieved and less stressed out.

To make focusing easier, delete time-consuming social media apps for a certain period of time. For example, every month, delete social media apps for six days. This gives you a nice break so you can focus on other things and not have your life consumed by social media.

But what if I feel like I'm going to miss out if I delete these apps?

Here's my take on this: Social media apps are good to use sometimes. But it shouldn't be the only thing you do when you have free time. Remember, your most valuable thing as a kid is your time advantage, so if you're just giving away that time for free, you are throwing away your advantage. I'm not telling you to just work hard and not have fun, but when you have free time, it's better to spend that time creating memories with friends and family, trying out new hobbies, and just doing new and exciting things. There is so much more to life than scrolling through social media!

So what if you don't see a photo or two your friends post? You'll benefit a lot more if you take that time and put it into doing more important and more fun things.

Whenever I decide to delete a social media app to focus more, I write down my username and password somewhere so I can log back into my account if I need to. Doing this gives me some peace of mind.

So what should I do with my free time now if I deleted these social media apps?

That's a great question. I would recommend using this time for doing any of these activities below:

- First, make sure all your important tasks are done first. This could be like doing homework, preparing for a tryout, etc.
- Create memories with your friends and loved ones. For example, you can play board games with them.
- Exercise! Many kids today don't get enough physical activity. Find a way to exercise if you don't do it already.
- Pick up some hobbies. You can learn to fish, drive a go-kart, go bike riding, learn to cook like a pro, go swimming, etc.

- **M**ake friends and socialize with new people. Ask yourself, how can I meet new people? One method could be to ask a couple of your current friends to introduce you to their friends. Maybe try to meet new people in school by talking to everyone in your class when you have a chance.
- **P**ick something you want to become better at. For example, how to get people to like you more, how to study faster, how to negotiate better, etc. Once you've found something you want to improve in, either read books or watch videos on the subject, then apply the info you learn! This is something a lot of successful people did to help them become successful. It's important that you believe you can improve at whatever you want to improve. I believe that you can definitely improve in different parts of life like socializing, selling, and memory if you educate yourself on the topic and take action on the information learned.
- **A**nd so much more!

Another way to stop spending a lot of time on social media is to set screen time limits. For example, social media apps are set to only 15 minutes a day. Many phones have this feature. Search up how you can do it on your device. This is a great way to make sure you are keeping track of your time. Adding to this, turn off social media notifications. They can distract you from staying focused.

Get your priorities in check. For example, there should be no reason to play video games when you should study for an upcoming test or work on that business you've been thinking about.

There are two different types of focus I like to think about. Focused focus (working for a set period of time with no distractions). And distracted focus (working with no set period of time set and having distractions around like a phone). When you have to do a task, always go with focused focus. Why? You'll finish whatever you're doing faster and with better quality.

In the picture above, we see that with focused work you get things done a lot faster, leaving you with more time to relax at the end. Next time you have to focus, use the

Pomodoro method mentioned above. You'll notice the difference in productivity.

Once you build powerful habits, they become second nature, and it won't be as hard to do these things. Putting your phone/electronic devices somewhere far away and shutting them off will feel less painful the more you do it, especially when you see how much you can get done without the distractions!

If you have absolutely nothing to do and want to relax, that's okay because we all need to relax sometimes. But we just can't relax when we have important things to get done first. From my experience, I like YouTube the most out of all the other social media platforms. You can learn about almost anything on YouTube. For example, there could be a YouTuber you watch that makes you laugh. That's something good to watch in your free time. There could also be a YouTuber that teaches about the subject you're interested in (for example, business, cars, or cooking). For the most part, when you do decide to relax, spend your time watching videos that are benefiting you, whether that benefit is laughter or learning. I usually avoid videos that are just entertaining that don't have a true benefit. I see those kinds of videos as a waste of time since I am not learning anything and I am not laughing.

The Importance of Sleep:

Most of the time, before I found self-development, I would come to school super tired without any energy and just anxiously waiting for the bell to ring so I could go home and take a nap. This is a common problem many kids have. They just come to school too tired.

Having more energy could make your life a lot better. So what's one of the easiest ways to get more energy?

Sleep! You have to create good sleeping habits, especially when you're young. Here are some key strategies you can use to make sleep your best friend:

Humans just don't function as well on little sleep. It's extremely important to get the recommended amount of sleep based on your age.

How much sleep you need by age:

Preteens: 9-12 hours

Teens: about 8-10 hours

Link to article: kidshealth.org/en/parents/sleep.html

Getting the recommended amount of sleep is easier when you wake up and go to bed at the same time. Your body gets used to the routine, and it is really good for you. A good sleep schedule is also going to improve your health.

Here's my challenge for you. Try to go to bed and wake up at the same time every day for two weeks. I know that it may be hard, but you'll notice the difference in sleep quality. By going to bed and waking at the same time, you'll feel more energized and ready to take on the day.

A lot of people argue, "I don't have time to get enough sleep! My schedule is too busy!" It's famously known that Jeff Bezos, founder of Amazon and one of the richest men on earth, gets on average 8 hours of sleep every night. Chances are, you're not busier than Jeff Bezos. If he's able to find time for 8 hours of sleep, chances are you can too!

Other than that, some other things I do to improve my sleep include:

- Taking hot showers before bed
- Doing a sleep meditation from the Headspace app
- Doing some sort of exercise during the day

For my alarm, I use this app called Sleep Cycle, and basically, this app tracks your sleeping patterns and wakes you up when you are in your lightest sleep phase. I started using this app about a year ago, and I would say that it's changed my life for the better. Ever since I began to use this app, I feel more energized compared to when I used a normal alarm clock.

Reading:

For most of my life, I had trouble reading. I wasn't the best reader, and I just felt that I couldn't read well in general. If you feel this way, don't give up on reading. One way you can improve your reading speed is to practice. I also highly recommend looking up videos on YouTube on how to improve your reading comprehension. They can be very helpful.

If you just hate reading books altogether, something I can recommend to do is to listen to audiobooks. I've learned that I personally can understand information a lot better when I'm listening to it, and you could be the same way! So the next time you need to read a book, try listening to the audio version. You may find out that you're a better auditory learner.

When I do decide to listen to an audiobook, I typically go to Audible. Sometimes some audiobooks aren't available on Audible. In those scenarios, use an app called Speechify. With Speechify, you take photos of the pages from the book, and it reads it to you!

Life:

Here's the thing. In life, you're going to have to do a lot of things you don't want to do but will eventually pay off in the long term.

Keep this idea in mind if you ever feel unmotivated: The feeling of discipline is a lot better than the feeling of regret. Discipline basically means to stick with your plan even though you may not feel like sticking with your plan. With regret, you can't do anything about it. That ship has sailed. For example: let's say you have a test you don't want to study for. You can either study or not study. If you choose not to study, you'll most likely regret it since you'll probably get a bad grade. But if you do study, even though you might not enjoy the time you spent studying, you'll be happier when you get your test back. Sometimes we have to do things we don't want to do to achieve a certain goal.

The example above shows the story of two different people. One person who did enter the video editing competition and one person who didn't enter it. Even though the person that won didn't enjoy the time they spent working on it, it all paid off in the end.

Three quick tips for life:

Quick tip 1: In today's world, many of us are on screens for most of the day. Here are some ways to help your eyes handle all the screen time. I like to use the

20-20-20 rule when I am using electronic devices. For every 20 minutes I look at the screen, I stop and look at something 20 feet away for 20 seconds, then repeat. Another thing that has really helped me is turning on blue light filters on my electronic devices. When you turn on blue light filters on your electronic devices, it filters out blue light that is bad for your eyes if looked at for too long, especially at night. After doing these things, my eyes feel a lot better overall. I have also started to sleep better ever since I began to use blue light filters on my devices.

Quick tip 2: Finding who you are as a person is an important thing that can help guide you to do the things that'll make you the happiest. That's why I recommend for everybody to take The 16 Personalities Test. Once you get the result, read the description of your personality. Your personality description will tell you things such as if you're a more introverted person or more of an extroverted person and more. If you're more of an introverted person, you enjoy spending time by yourself more. If you're more of an extroverted person, you enjoy spending time socializing with others more. You can also be a combination of both. It's important to know what you are so you can spend your time doing what makes you the happiest.

Take the personality test at:
16personalities.com

Quick tip 3: Have a to-do list filled with things you need to do for the day. Having a to-do list helps me remember important things I have to do. You can also include breaks in your to-do list if you like. I highly recommend using a to-do list. You can buy a small whiteboard with some dry erase markers from the store and fill up the list with things you need to do for the next day. It's always best to fill out your list the night before so you can have a set schedule for the next day.

To end off this chapter:

A YouTuber Kelly Wakasa always says: "Do what excites." I love that quote because it can push you to do new and exciting things in life. Do what excites you! Does it sound fun to join the soccer team? Then do it! Does it sound fun to go to a summer camp? Then do it! Does it sound fun to start a YouTube channel? Then do it! Do what excites you! Within limitations, of course, don't do anything illegal or something that could get you into trouble.

Chapter 3:

Friends

You may have heard about the idea that the people you hang out with most often influence what you will be like in the future. From personal experience, I can tell you that this is 100% true.

> **"You are the average of the five people you spend the most time with."**
>
> **—Jim Rohn**

We humans tend to follow what the other humans around us do. That's just human nature. If you are hanging out with a group of friends that have bad habits and do drugs, chances are you will eventually have bad habits and do drugs.

To find friends that are overall good people, you may have to branch out of your comfort zone and introduce yourself to new people. So if you're looking for some new friends, take the initiative and introduce yourself to new people whenever you have the chance. This means that you probably will have to be the one that starts the conversation. Is there a new kid sitting next to you in class? Get to know them! Is there a group project you're doing with people you don't know? Get to know them! Try to talk to as many people as possible! Get to know everyone! You can make some fantastic friends this way! It may be difficult introducing yourself to somebody new, but the more you do it, the easier it can become.

Drifting away from bad friends:

Sometimes you may find yourself being friends with troublemakers and just not good people in general. By drifting away from them, it could cause them to change and stop doing bad things like bullying or using drugs to be friends with you again. Don't be afraid to drift away from bad friends. Hanging out with the wrong group of friends can ruin your life. A bad group of friends will bring you down and stop you from advancing in life. If you somehow end up being friends with troublemakers, use the strategy below.

The Drift Away Strategy:

The first step to this is to make sure you have other friends before cutting someone off. If you don't, try to make new friends first by introducing yourself to as many people as possible. This way, you won't be lonely after cutting them off. Basically, what you want to do is slowly and steadily stop being friends with whoever you would like to cut off. First, start off by not hanging out with them outside of school. Next, try to talk to them less and less in school. If they say hi to you in school, there's no problem with saying hi back. Just avoid hanging out with them outside of school and try to talk to them very little or not at all.

When using this strategy, whoever you are trying to cut off may ask you: "Why can't you hangout or do anything anymore?" There are two different ways you can answer this.

The first way to answer this is to say: "I've just been really busy."

Chances are, in response, they're going to say: "Busy doing what?" Be prepared to answer that. Whether your answer is going to be soccer practice, football practice, or just that you have to spend time with family, be ready with a good response.

The second way you can answer this is by being straight to the point with your reason. For example: "Look, the reason why I don't want to hangout with you anymore is that you (insert reason here)." Your reason can be because they do drugs, it could be that they are very rude to others, because they are a bad influence in general, etc. Using this way to answer the question "Why can't you hangout anymore?" is good because it can cause the other person to change from doing bad things to become friends with you again. But in many cases, they won't change from doing bad things, and that's okay because now you know that you definitely shouldn't be friends with them.

In general, a good rule to keep in mind is to not hangout with people that have bad habits and don't have goals for their life. Hangout with the people who have good hobbies. Hangout with the people that are nice to others and good people in general.

If you're looking to make new friends, really take every opportunity you can get to talk to people. Talk to everyone in your class and get to know them. Even talk to the kids others may call "losers" or "nerds" because if you get to know them, they could be amazing people.

Chapter 4

Losing hope

Sometimes, life can seriously get tough.

If you're feeling hopeless, or just lost in general, look forward to your future and the things you plan to do in the future. Then think about what steps you can take in your life to make your goals become a reality, whether those are steps you have to take today or in the future.

There are so many amazing people you haven't met yet that could turn your life upside down in a positive way. There are so many awesome things you haven't done yet. And there are so many new pieces of technology coming out in the future that will be amazing.

The National Suicide Hotline is an excellent place to talk to somebody about how you feel. They are available 24/7, for free, and they offer completely confidential support. If you feel like you are losing hope, grab a phone and go somewhere where nobody can hear you, then call the hotline. It may very well give you a lot of new hope in life. Their number is **1-800-273-8255.**

If you would like to have a text conversion with somebody instead, you can go to:

crisistextline.org

Please, seek professional help if you feel like you need it. There are people that dedicate their whole lives to help people thinking about suicide, to provide support when people need it.

> "Most of the important things in the world have been accomplished by people who kept on trying when there seemed to be no hope at all."
>
> —Dale Carnegie

Chapter 5:

Drugs

In this chapter, I use the word recreational a few times. Recreational means for fun and enjoyment.

In my opinion, this is the most important chapter in the book because the stuff you learn in this chapter can prevent you from a lifetime of drug addiction.

Just think about it for a second. There are probably so many goals that people didn't accomplish because of drugs. So many businesses not started, so many places not traveled to, so many career paths that weren't pursued, the list goes on and on.

The first time many people take a drug, it may seem harmless, but it can lead to terrible things you never would think you would do.

Why you should avoid drugs:

There are no solid benefits for using drugs recreationally due to their downsides. And whatever benefits some people may talk about, you can get the same benefits from something safer. Some people argue that, for example, weed makes them sleep better. If you're looking for a way to sleep better, you can do things like drink chamomile tea, do a sleep meditation, exercise more throughout the day, and so much more. Some people argue that they enjoy vaping because of the different flavors. Instead of vaping, you can go to a local bakery and buy some of the most delicious cakes and candy. Some people argue that it is "cool" to smoke. If it's the "cool" part you're looking for. There are many other things that are a lot better than that. For example, electric scooters and electric bikes are a blast to ride (just remember to wear a helmet). If your whole friend group buys an electric scooter or bike, you guys can ride together and have a ton of fun. Or do something even cooler like starting a business. The possibilities are endless!

If it's the fun you're looking for, there are better things you can do for fun, maybe go-karting, bowling, skiing, etc. Maybe search up on google what some fun things are that people your age can do.

Suppose you're doing drugs because of friends pressuring you. In that case, you shouldn't hang out with those people because those people that are pressuring others to do drugs aren't going to be good people in the future, most likely. Those people likely become very miserable and possibly homeless when they're older. The people that want to pressure you to do drugs usually don't have any goals for their own life, so they try to bring others down with them. Stay away from these people.

At the end of the day, it really doesn't make sense to do any recreational drugs because there is too much of a downside and an upside that you can get from safer things. Becoming addicted to a drug is a serious thing that can make you depressed, anxious, and lose all motivation in life.

Suppose we look at all of the recreational drug overdoses in the history of the world. If all these people who overdosed decided to say no to drugs every single time, there would be no overdoses from recreational drugs. That's the power of saying no. A simple no can save your life.

A lot of people tell themselves: "I'll try this drug once, and I won't do it again." But in many cases, they end up trying other drugs and becoming addicted, all from trying a drug once. You can prevent a lifetime of addiction by simply deciding to never try them.

How to avoid drugs:

The first thing is to never put yourself in situations where you get offered drugs. So, for example, if you get invited to a party, and you know there's going to be drugs there, you shouldn't go because they're going to pressure you to do these things, even if you think that they won't. The second tactic is to simply say no if you are ever offered drugs. You can combine saying no with one of the many excuses I have listed below. And remember becoming a drug addict all starts from trying it once, so don't let anybody fool you into trying a drug one time.

Excuses to tell people that try peer pressuring you to do drugs:

- "I have asthma, and this will mess up my lungs."
- "I can't share any vapes or marijuana with you because I have a disease. My doctor told me not to share anything where your lips have to touch unless you want to get infected." If you decide to use this excuse, look upon the internet different names of diseases so if somebody asks, "What disease do you have?" you can answer them.
- Say that you aren't trying to mess up your life. Tell them that you have actual goals other than sitting around and looking for a way to get entertained.
- Say something like: "I can't. My parents drug test me once a week since they're concerned about the things I do. I'll get into a lot of trouble if I test positive on the drug test." Using your parents as an excuse is something others will likely understand.
- Say that you're highly allergic to whatever drug you are being offered. For example: "I'm allergic to weed."
- Say that you're on a team (for example, soccer or football team) and that your coach drug tests

everyone once a week. For example: "I can't, I'm on this soccer team, and my coach drug tests us all once a week. If I test positive for drugs, I'll get kicked out of my team."

After using one or more of these excuses to say no to drugs, leave the place, go, do not stay under any circumstance. Don't talk to these people again unless they change. Because if you still keep in contact with people that do things like drugs and continue to hang out with them, you will eventually become one of them, and your entire future can get messed up.

If you ever use one of these excuses, be confident in your answer. When you're confident about your answer, it makes it seem more believable.

An example where using an excuse worked:

I was at a middle school party with a few friends, not expecting anyone to bring or use any drugs since we were all so young. After some time, one person pulls out a vape from their backpack, and they begin to pass it around. When I saw the vape, I had a feeling that it would not be good if I tried it, so I had to find a way to get out of being pressured into trying it. I told everyone that I had to go to the bathroom right before the vape got passed to me. Instead of going to the bathroom, I found the main door and left without saying goodbye to anyone. I walked to the entrance of the neighborhood and texted my dad to pick me up. After about 10 minutes, he arrived, and I felt so relieved after getting in his car. I successfully avoided drugs that day. Sometimes you have to do creative things like that to avoid drugs.

Parties:

When I'm talking about a high school party, I'm talking about a party where there's no parental supervision, usually at someone's home.

High school parties are a waste of time. High school parties are where many people try drugs for the first time then eventually become addicted. There are so many more fun things you could do instead of going to a high school party. You could go for a relaxing drive (if you have your license), you can go go-karting, you could go try new foods at different restaurants, you could go to cool stores, you could get a job to make money for yourself, you could start a business to make money for yourself, you can look up fun and exciting things for people your age to do, you can look up fun things to do in your local area. There are so many more fun things you could do.

Be careful about going to a party at somebody's home, especially when there will be no parents to supervise. If you get invited to a party at home, I would first ask if there will be parents there. If no parents will be there, do not go at all, it's not worth it. If there are parents there to be safe, ask around what will be going on at the party. Is everybody planning to go to a secret room to do drugs or try alcohol? If so, skip the party. You can usually get these kinds of questions answered if you ask people that are going there.

A good rule to keep in mind is to be very, very careful about house parties. Birthday parties at, for example, restaurants, arcades, and bowling alleys are perfectly fine to go to. Those are good parties since there's almost never anything like drugs involved and you can have a good time with your friends.

Below I talk about why two of the most popular drugs used by middle schoolers and high schoolers are not good:

Why Vaping is not good:

When you do something like vaping, you rewire your brain to become addicted to vaping. It just becomes a habit after a little bit of time. Most vapes have this thing in them called nicotine. What nicotine does is basically tricks your brain into becoming addicted.

According to kidshealth.org, nicotine can:

- Affect your ability to remember things
- Affect your ability to concentrate properly
- Make it harder to learn new things
- Make the chances higher that you'll become addicted to other drugs in life

Link to article: kidshealth.org/en/teens/e-cigarettes. html

Nicotine-free vapes are popular because some people think they're safe due to them not having nicotine. But that's simply not the case. Scientists haven't looked into these kinds of vapes enough to see the possible long-term effects. And with the studies done so far on nicotine-free vaping, they don't look good. Scientists today recommend that it's best for kids to avoid all kinds of vaping.

Vaping can also cause serious damage to your lungs due to the chemicals in them.

Why weed is not good:

Now keep in mind the argument I'm making against weed is for the average kid or teenager. If your doctor or medical professional is telling you to use weed for some sort of medical reason, it is okay to use it. Here is why weed you should never use it for recreational reasons:

Link to the article with some of the main points are below:

drugfreeworld.org/drugfacts/marijuana/short-and-long-term-effects.html

Short term effects of weed:

- Short-term issues with your memory
- Severe anxiety, which includes a fear that you're being watched or followed by someone
- Seeing, hearing, or smelling different things that aren't actually there
- A slower reaction time
- Issues with your coordination

Long term effects of weed:

- Decline in IQ
- Bad performance in school and an increased chance of dropping out of school
- Your thinking and ability to learn and complete harder tasks is lowered
- Lower overall fulfillment in life
- Higher chances of becoming jobless or not getting a good job in general

Is this what you want in life? No, nobody does. But the sad truth is many get tricked into doing a drug once, and they never end up quitting then later moving on to even more harmful drugs. Getting stuck in a never-ending cycle of addiction.

So how about instead of spending hundreds of dollars a month on drugs, alcohol, and pointless things like that, go and lease or buy a cool car like a Mazda Miata. With the Mazda Miata, you'll get something that's enjoyable to drive. But here's the thing: driving a fun car like the Mazda Miata won't ruin your life the way as drugs can. It may very well improve it because it can make you a happier person in general since you'll have something awesome to look forward to. At the same time, it's a form of transportation you can actually use to get places. So when you turn driving age, consider taking the money that you would have possibly spent on drugs and spend it towards an awesome car. It just gives you such an advantage over everybody else when you're not doing drugs.

As a teenager, you can work a job that'll make you your own money and put that money towards a fun car. That's what I would recommend you do, get a job as a teenager (or start a business), spend a certain amount of money a month on a cool car, then save or invest everything else.

Doing yourself a favor:

The process of having to quit a drug is terrible. You'll go through withdrawals, and you won't feel good altogether. So do yourself a favor and just say no if you are ever offered. If you somehow end up in a situation where you are offered drugs, I would recommend using some of the excuses I listed above around the start of this chapter. When you say no to drugs, you're saying yes to the best version of yourself. You're saying yes to making your dreams come true. You're saying yes to making your family glad. So a simple no to drugs turns into a lot of good things. It may be uncomfortable to say no to drugs when you're in the moment, but you'll feel so good after you've successfully said no to drugs and left the situation. Your time is truly priceless as a kid/teenager; many people would pay insane amounts of money to be a kid/teen again. So with this precious resource you have, time, don't put it to waste by creating an addiction for yourself.

Some potential ways you can quit drugs if you are already addicted:

1st way: Set a date to quit (for example, 30 days from now). Then reduce your drug intake slowly and steadily until you reach your quit date. Once you reach your quit date, stop your drug intake. This method requires self-discipline to complete successfully but has proven to work for many people.

2nd way: Tell a trusted friend or family member about your addiction and see if they can keep you accountable to make sure you never do drugs again. Give them all the drugs you are addicted to and have them throw it all away. It may be hard to talk about drug use with a loved one, but by doing it, you could put an end to your addiction.

3rd way:
Go to teen.smokefree.gov for resources on how you can quit smoking or vaping.

For any other substances you may be addicted to, call the Substance Abuse and Mental Health Services Administration at **1-800-662-4357**.

Friend groups:

There's a group of kids in many schools known as the "popular" group. The people in this "popular" group could be great people, but at the same time, they may be troublemakers. Many people hold this "popular" group to a very high level. And some get tricked into taking drugs after being told by a "popular" person to do the drug. When it comes to popular and unpopular kids, just take that idea out of your mind. Treat everybody with respect. We are all humans. Maybe there's a kid that other kids think of as "unpopular" but if you get to know them, they may just be an amazing person.

There's a famous quote from Bill Gates I really like: "Be nice to nerds. Chances are you'll end up working for one." So keep in mind that if these "popular" kids are doing bad things, not keeping good habits, not being kind to others, they are likely not going to be popular when they're older. Chances are, if they're doing things like that, they'll be miserable and living a bad life when they're older.

The only people that you should keep in high regard are successful people. Those are the people you should look up to and learn from, not some random "popular" kid at school. People like Bill Gates and Jeff Bezos, the list goes on and on.

There's no benefit to finding a way to fit in with a group of kids that do bad things like drugs. It doesn't matter if the people in your school think they're cool. The honest truth is that their opinions aren't important if they think hanging out with people that do bad things like drugs is cool.

If the popular group of kids happen to be good people, and they don't do bad things like drugs, there's no problem hanging out with them. But in general, hang out with the kids who have their priorities straight and have goals for their lives, not the kids who are just "cool" because they do bad things.

Don't think of the "popular" group as higher than you because if they're doing things such as drugs and other bad things, they're not on a higher level than you. You're actually on a higher level than them if they're the ones doing bad things like drugs and you are not. In that case, you would be setting yourself up for success, and they're setting themselves up for failure.

The actual popular people are the people that are successful in life, whether that's a football player in the NFL, a basketball player in the NBA, or a billionaire businessman. Those are the popular people you should look up to, not the "popular" group in school.

Resources that show the harm of some commonly used drugs:

This link for vaping and smoking:
Therealcost.betobaccofree.hhs.gov

This link for weed:
drugfreeworld.org/drugfacts/marijuana/short-and-long-term-effects.html

This link for alcohol:
drugfreeworld.org/drugfacts/alcohol/short-term-long-term-effects.html

Avoid recreational drugs. Find other, more important (and more fun) things to do.

This was mentioned earlier in the book, but it deserves to be mentioned a second time. Suppose we look at all of the recreational drug overdoses in the history of the world. If all these people who overdosed decided to say no to drugs every single time, there would be no overdoses from recreational drugs. That's the power of saying no. A simple no can save your life.

Chapter 6

The Conclusion:

So here's my conclusion of all of this:

- **S**tay away from drugs for recreational purposes. They can take away your focus, time, and money.
- **A**ssociate with the right people, be careful with who you hang out with. And if you do find yourself in the wrong crowd, use the "drift away strategy" in chapter three to leave that group of friends.
- **U**se the focus and sleep techniques in chapter two.
- **S**tart getting some exercise throughout the day if you don't already (it's really good for you).
- **T**ake the 16 personalities quiz to learn more about yourself. 16personalities.com.
- **A**nd do what excites you! Sometimes you have to take risks to make awesome things happen!

Tools that future successful people use:

- Books

- Informational videos
- Good sleep
- Good friends

Tools that future unsuccessful people use:

- Drugs
- Bad sleep
- Bad friends
- Activities that waste your time

That's it. I believe that if you avoid recreational drugs, hang out with good people, and have good habits overall. You're set to create the best version of yourself.

Three books I highly recommend that are amazing for personal development:

- Managing Oneself by Peter F. Drucker
- How to Win Friends and Influence People by Dale Carnegie
- Sell or Be Sold by Grant Cardone

Now go out there, do what excites you, and create the very best version of yourself with the information you learned in this book!

References:

Chapter 2:

Francesco Cirillo, "The Pomodoro Technique," Cirillo Consulting, francescocirillo.com/pages/pomodoro-technique.

Raptitude. "How to Work Now and Procrastinate Later." Raptitude.com, 2 Apr. 2014, www.raptitude.com/2014/02/procrastinate-later/.

Mayo Clinic Staff. "7 Great Reasons Why Exercise Matters." Mayo Clinic, Mayo Foundation for Medical Education and Research, 11 May 2019, www.mayoclinic.org/healthy-lifestyle/fitness/in-depth/exercise/art-20048389.

"All About Sleep (for Parents) - Nemours KidsHealth." Reviewed by Elana Pearl Ben-Joseph, KidsHealth, The Nemours Foundation, June 2019, kidshealth.org/en/parents/sleep.html.

National Sleep Foundation. "What Is Circadian Rhythm / Body Clock?" Sleep.org, 19 Oct. 2020, www.sleep.org/circadian-rhythm-body-clock/.

National Sleep Foundation. "How to Design a Nighttime Routine." Sleep.org, 23 Jan. 2020, www.sleep.org/design-perfect-bedtime-routine/.

Nall, Rachel. "20-20-20 Rule: How to Prevent Eye Strain." Reviewed by Ann Marie Griff, Medical News Today, Healthline Media, www.medicalnewstoday.com/articles/321536.

Chapter 5:

"Vaping: What You Need to Know (for Teens) - Nemours KidsHealth." Reviewed by Lonna P. Gordon, KidsHealth, The Nemours Foundation, Sept. 2019, kidshealth.org/en/teens/e-cigarettes.html.

Johnson, Jon. "Side Effects of Vaping without Nicotine." Reviewed by Kevin Martinez, Medical News Today, 27 Sept. 2019, www.medicalnewstoday.com/articles/326489#effects.

Vapes: Product Page - The Real Cost, therealcost. betobaccofree.hhs.gov/vapes.

"Short- & Long-Term Effects of Marijuana - Negative Side Effects of Weed - Drug-Free World." Foundation for a Drug-Free World, www.drugfreeworld.org/drugfacts/marijuana/short-and-long-term-effects.html.

Ellgren, Maria. "Neurobiological Effects of Early Life Cannabis Exposure in Relation to the Gateway Hypothesis." KI Open Archive Home, Institutionen

För Klinisk neurovetenskap / Department of Clinical Neuroscience, 9 Feb. 2007, openarchive.ki.se/xmlui/handle/10616/38245.

National Institute on Drug Abuse. "Is Marijuana a Gateway Drug?" National Institute on Drug Abuse, 8 Apr. 2020, www.drugabuse.gov/publications/research-reports/marijuana/marijuana-gateway-drug.

Phillips, Leigh. "Drop in IQ Linked to Heavy Teenage Cannabis Use." Nature News, Nature Publishing Group, 28 Aug. 2012, www.nature.com/news/drop-in-iq-linked-to-heavy-teenage-cannabis-use-1.11278.

NIDA. "How does marijuana produce its effects?." National Institute on Drug Abuse, 8 Apr. 2020, https://www.drugabuse.gov/publications/research-reports/marijuana/how-does-marijuana-produce-its-effects.

University of California - Davis Health System. "Heavy, persistent pot use linked to economic, social problems at midlife: Study finds marijuana not 'safer' than alcohol." ScienceDaily. ScienceDaily, 23 March 2016. <www.sciencedaily.com/releases/2016/03/160323082016.htm>.

Weir, K. (2015, November). Marijuana and the developing brain. Monitor on Psychology, 46(10). http://www.apa.org/monitor/2015/11/marijuana-brain

NIDA. "Is marijuana safe and effective as medicine?." National Institute on Drug Abuse, 21 Oct. 2020, https://www.drugabuse.gov/publications/research-reports/marijuana/marijuana-safe-effective-medicine.

Meier, Madeline H, et al. "Persistent Cannabis Users Show Neuropsychological Decline from Childhood to Midlife." PNAS, National Academy of Sciences, 2 Oct. 2012, www.pnas.org/content/109/40/E2657.full.

Nichols, Hannah. "Five Ways to Quit Smoking." Medical News Today, MediLexicon International, www.medicalnewstoday.com/articles/319460.